PAMELA L. HEWLETT

Wedding Planning: The Glam &
The Glum
Vol. I

A Collage of Thoughts & Experiences from a
Wedding Planner

The events and conversations in this book have been set down to the best of the author's ability, although some names and details have been changed to protect the privacy of individuals.

Cover Design: iCatcha Design

Glam:
Sass, panache, and a dash of happy
Adjective: Glamorous

Glum:
Looking or feeling dejected; morose
Adjective: Gloomy

A Collage of Thoughts & Experiences from a
Wedding Planner

This book is dedicated to my mother, Lessie M. Hewlett, because, well, she's my Mama. Most importantly, though, she was the one who took me to my very first gala, which was held at the United Center in Chicago. I was a second-year scholarship recipient for an organization she once worked with. It was there where I first laid eyes upon bright oversized "day-of" stationery. It was there where I twirled in the middle of the elaborate foyer, which was smothered in sparkly gold and ivory pipe and drape. It was a vision to see, but what I remember most is how much joy everyone seemed to feel. People of all ages and races were gathered together and everyone was just happy. It was the most beautiful thing I had ever seen. I departed the gala, body exhausted and mind excited with wonder and awe. I talked about the event all the way home and for the next several weeks. It was then that I knew I had found it. I was in a space that I knew I wanted to come back to over and over again. For that, I am forever grateful.

Thank you, Mama!

Table Of Contents

Hi, there!

These thoughts were recorded with the aspiring, the new, and the seasoned wedding planner in mind. I have had the pleasure of being a party to every category. Penning this book has been on my heart for some time now. I'd never lacked the ability to say what others wouldn't until the idea of writing this book consistently invaded my thoughts. I contemplated the idea in my head yearly, monthly, weekly, and then daily, until earlier this year, when I could no longer keep my thoughts under wraps. I released my self-doubt, external doubt, and procrastination and put my pen to pad. I have just begun and with caution to the wind, it is such an exhilarating moment to have even completed my first paragraph. It's funny that I waited all this time to get started. But, now that I have, I find myself already brainstorming ideas and determining what should be saved for book number two!

I love wedding planning so supremely, I cannot truly place it into words. Owning my own wedding planning business has afforded me the pleasure of experiencing it all. When we love something so much, we are sometimes afraid to be transparent about the things we may not love about it. Some wedding planners are often afraid to share the challenges associated with running a wedding planning business because we don't want to be perceived by clients as an inexperienced wedding professional, by peers as a negative colleague, or by those who don't even know us as a failure. The truth is we have no control over any of this. My dad has experienced some health challenges, and when I speak to him, I am amazed at his positive outlook on his health. He often says, "Well, Pam, if I'm going to tell you about the bad days, it's only fair that I call you and share the excitement of my good days too." Countering each negative with a positive can help to create a healthy balance in your thinking.

Social media often glorifies being a wedding planner—or being a small business owner in any industry. It is so easy to share the Glam parts of wedding planning, often making it appear as if the Glum parts don't exist. Smiling at the gorgeous end result is the easy part. The journey to get there though . . . that's the part we don't publicly share and the part that others don't have an opportunity to experience before diving into this industry headfirst. I believe it would be a disservice to myself as well as aspiring wedding planners to not bare some of my "wedding planning" soul.

I have been blessed to create and bring to life weddings for some of the most amazing clients on the planet. I am extremely proud of every single one of them. I believe that sharing perspectives and experiences at any stage of your career as a wedding planner can always be of help to someone else. We don't have to wait until we have retired from the industry, or have ten thousand social media followers, to share our thoughts and experiences in a book or speech. I hope to write an amazing book when I have retired and have many more stories to share, but there's no rule that says I have to wait that long.

Like with anything, not everyone will agree with or love every sentence or scenario I share here. Some will laugh. Some may even cry (happy tears, I hope). Some may not be pleased with the idea that I've spilled some of the wedding industry "tea," or faux pas, if you will. Some might deem me unfit to serve in this industry or declare me as unhappy with my own business, and that's okay. Lastly, and most importantly, some might feel inspired to write the books that have been living inside of their hearts for years.

Some might finally start that wedding planning business. Some might read this and realize they aren't alone. This is not a how-to book. My truest desire is to help someone else. To all individual interpretations—with love, here are my thoughts.

Best,

Pamela

Chapter 1

SO, You Want to Be a Wedding Planner?

Many of us at some point during our careers as wedding planners still work full-time jobs. Most of the time, our clients are not aware of this because, at some juncture, we have managed to master the art of balance and concealment. Whether you choose to share this knowledge with clients or not is truly your own personal preference. Previously, and rather early on, I chose to share this information with my clients. Although they had never experienced any major setbacks or delays, due to time constraints with my formal, full-time employer, I shared my other work commitments with clients in an effort to set realistic expectations where my availability was concerned. I also wanted to build trust. Each client I chose to share it with was very understanding and even grateful that I was so open with them. As my business continued to grow and I gained more experience with balancing two jobs and communicating consistently, it became no longer necessary to disclose my other employment obligations.

One must possess exceptional multitasking skills and communication abilities to maintain two employment obligations under the guise of only one. This is especially important for small business owners when your main client base consists of brides and grooms-to-be. I've watched friends in the wedding industry crumble and have to close up shop simply because they weren't honest about their true abilities. They weren't honest with themselves—and therefore their clients—regarding the true level of commitment that they could actually provide. In other words, some wedding professionals overcommit themselves and make it seem as if they have more availability or capacity than they really have. As a result of this over-promising and under-delivering, I have had to sever business ties with some friends in the industry on more occasions than I care to recall. Whatever stage you are in, I implore you to be very careful and discerning about building relationships in your business. Very often, when stuff (you know what word I really mean here . . .) hits the fan, some of those wedding-industry friends of yours will ghost you, even when they are the very ones who deposited you into the middle of a fire with your client. Wedding planners are at the front, center, and end of every single detail and component of a wedding. If a bride and groom hire a wedding planner, they are not concerned with the details their other wedding vendors missed, but they will be concerned with the details their paid wedding planner failed to communicate to each vendor.

To be successful, you must build strong, healthy, consistent relationships. When I was still very green to wedding planning, I wondered why some wedding planners seemed to consistently use the same set of vendors for each of their events. I thought I was doing something really grand by scouting a completely different set of vendors for each new wedding. Really, all I was doing was creating unnecessary additional work for myself. Please understand that every vendor isn't a perfect match for every client, so you will need to constantly work to build relationships with wedding vendors. However, I learned that there is great value in using something that works, and that it is okay to build a dream team (or two or three) of wedding vendors.

We have all made mistakes in entrepreneurship, which is okay because after we correct and recover from them, we experience growth. It is extremely valuable to be able to self-evaluate. This helps us to always be in tune with our role. Self-evaluation helps us to clearly determine the role that we as the entrepreneur and business owner may have played in the setbacks, mistakes, and losses that we experience in our businesses. Self-evaluation at any point, both personally and professionally, can be our greatest asset.

I have many wedding-planner and wedding-industry friends and associates whose sole job is to manage their wedding businesses. These individuals have invested countless hours into acquiring the necessary resources and building the proper relationships needed to shape and equip those small businesses with the tools it takes to succeed and survive. Few in the wedding industry have started successful wedding planning businesses without also balancing another job. Maintaining full-time employment at an organization, plus either starting, building, or maintaining a wedding planning business, is not for the faint of heart. It is hard, and there are a lot of tears involved. Oftentimes, that first wedding budget or wedding planning fee that you're paid isn't enough to encourage you to ever consider quitting your day job. Heck, sometimes it's not enough to make you want to do it all over again for client number two. As I write this, I know some of my seasoned wedding planners or wedding-industry professionals will find this comical because they remember this moment. You might be curled up on your couch with your favorite blanket, sipping a glass of wine that you nearly spit out because you can recall *exactly* how this feels—and the very individuals who made you feel it!

Being a part of the wedding planning industry is so much fun and my, my, my, do we all have some stories to tell. We love what we do but, on wedding day, when it's lights, camera, action, the pressure is on! We all work as a team to ensure that no detail goes unnoticed or uncorrected. Because it's such a busy day for a team of wedding vendors, I usually try to speak to all of my vendors who serviced a wedding with me within a few days after the event. I schedule those calls to recap and celebrate what did or didn't happen . . . things like how the top tier of the cake didn't actually topple over (when it really almost did) during delivery and transition. Or that the bride's veil didn't actually catch on fire (when it really almost did) after a guest knocked over some candles milliseconds after the bride strolled by. Oh, and one of my all-time favorites is when the DJ and I successfully hid the microphone from the unscheduled toast makers, like cousin so-and-so who wanted to share the funny stories about the double dates she and the bride used to go on, or from the groom's former roommate who wanted to recount those amazing times in college.

Remember this: The bride and groom are the super-stars of the wedding, but the wedding planner is expected to be the superstar at managing all of the details necessary to stage a full-service wedding. A wedding planner could potentially be tasked with the responsibility of communicating details between twenty-five vendors for one wedding at one time. It is the responsibility of the wedding planner to interpret the couple's visions and desires for everyone else. Until you've established your dream team of preferred wedding professionals, you may bump your head a little. You are almost sure to encounter vendors who will require more from you than your bride and groom. These are all growing pains that will contribute to the success of your business.

Valuable relationships are one of the most important assets you will ever have as a wedding planner. I am a wedding planner who likes to handle every single detail associated with my clients' weddings from beginning to end, so it is important to my business that I have relationships established with other detail-oriented wedding professionals. We always want to maintain a high level of professionalism, but the truth is, wedding planners and other wedding professionals don't always keep traditional office hours. Therefore, it is important to get to know a little about each person you work with. Find out who's most likely to burn the midnight oil with you or who you need to be sure to connect with before 6:00 p.m. Find your solid, reliable, relatable tribe, develop a sense of familiarity, and share an occasional meal with them. Work to build a mutual respect with one another. Do whatever you must to maintain a positive connection with each of them. This will help alleviate stress as well as allow you to have a little fun and enjoy your wedding planning business.

Chapter 2

Wedding Planner or Personal Assistant?

In this business—or in any business, for that matter—especially if you're an entrepreneur or small business owner, you will cross a road that will require you to ask yourself, Is this what I'm supposed to be doing? or Is this even what I want to be doing? Every business owner in almost every industry experiences an encounter that forces them to question if the business that they are sacrificing everything for, is even worth it. This does not mean that you don't love what you do or that you don't believe that you're good at what you do. It simply means you are human. These questions usually surface during or after challenging experiences or when the phone is not ringing with the prospect of new opportunities for your business.

I reached this point a little over seven years ago, after a destination wedding that I had worked on for approximately eight months. The overall experience caused me to shut down on wedding planning and the wedding industry for a little while. Do I love what I do? Absolutely! Am I passionate about it? Without a doubt! But I am also a real-life person who believes in morals, boundaries, peace of mind, and, most importantly, respect.

A couple hired Pamela Hewlett Events to plan their wedding. The couple was referred to me by a friend of the bride, who I previously volunteered with. The friend shared that the bride needed assistance because she was stressing out everyone around her about the details of her wedding—details they didn't feel comfortable taking on (Run, Pamela, RUN!). I had previously met the bride but I didn't really know her personally, and it had been a few years since I had interacted with her. Naively, I believed I could easily manage what I had come to identify as a "unique" personality. Both the future bride and groom had very demanding careers, taking the medical and legal fields by storm. They were also finding and moving into their first home together, planning a wedding, and juggling all of the things that come with building a new life together. After a number of venue visits, the couple decided that they'd rather marry on a beautiful secluded island surrounded by water. Once they settled on a gorgeous resort in Mexico for their destination wedding, plans were underway.

The First Red Flag . . . The Invitation Fiasco

The bride stressed that she was interested in the simplest of wedding invitations. Most of the stationery designers in today's wedding industry work digitally, which means they don't generally provide individual, physical samples unless they're from a previously completed project. It is far too costly for a stationer to design and present a physical mock-up of each potential design, especially for someone who's not yet formally hired them. In this particular instance, the bride was adamant about seeing samples in her color palette before agreeing to hire one of the designers I had recommended.

I have always been fortunate enough to develop beautiful, healthy relationships with every single one of our vendors. After some sweet-talking with one of the designers the bride seemed to be considering, she was kind enough to create some mock samples, in the couple's color palette, for them to review. The bride was not thrilled with any of the samples. It is absolutely okay for a bride to not love the initial design. This is for her big day, and we make every effort to ensure that our brides' visions come to fruition and that they receive the services they are paying for. This is also a good thing, because it helps both the designer and wedding planner get an idea of what a bride doesn't like or want. However, on a three-way call, the bride told the very kind and patient designer that the designs she had created were something the bride could have completed on her own computer. After both the designer and I asked a number of very specific probing questions, the bride unfortunately had difficulty verbalizing what she disliked or liked about each sample design, which would have aided us in knowing which direction to go.

Detailed communication between the couple, wedding planner, and stationery designer is extremely important. The wedding stationery often serves as one of the most important elements of the wedding planning process —the centerpiece and focal point for wedding planners and all other wedding vendors when they prepare each of their individual creative contributions to the wedding. Therefore, we need this part of the planning process, among others, to be as seamless as possible. Eventually, the designer and I were able to pull a little more inspiration from additional ideas the bride shared with us via a virtual vision board that we requested she create specifically for her wedding invitation. Then, after the stationery designer shared a few other design samples with her, we were able to create a design she was pleased with.

Since the couple contracted us in late fall, just before the holidays and the onset of a Midwest winter, both the save-the-date cards and invitations went out in the dead of winter. The idea for a foreign destination wedding was born because both the bride and groom had hosted huge weddings in their previous marriages. This time around, they both desired an intimate celebration away from the city. They planned to only invite their closest friends and family from near and far. The wedding was to be held in the summer of the following year.

When planning destination weddings, the timeline for each step looks different from weddings that take place locally. The invitations need to go out much sooner. I always advise clients to send the invitations out on or before January 1 of the year the wedding is scheduled to take place. (Yes, this means they should be printed by or before Christmas!) If not already planned, January is when most people plan their budgets, travel, and other activities for the year. It is also when individuals receive their new allotment of vacation days from their employers. With this advisement, I request that couples send me their guests' addresses almost immediately after they hire Pamela Hewlett Events. The contact information on the individuals listed in your cell phone usually only consists of phone numbers and maybe an email address. Therefore, it takes couples some time to complete their guest list and acquire the necessary information needed for addressing. Time must also be allotted for our stationery designers to design the guest addresses, and for our couples to proofread them, before sending everything to print. (Please note that this couple had opted for handwritten envelope addressing in calligraphy, so additional time had to be allotted to physically transfer the invitations to the calligrapher before they could be mailed out.)

Although I followed up almost daily and even offered to meet the couple so that I could manually input any handwritten addresses they had acquired—in an effort to speed the process along—the couple was extremely late in completing and submitting their guest address list to me. The winter holidays had come and gone. It was now the middle of January, and totals were due to our venue by the middle of April.

Finally, I received an email from the bride notifying me that their guest addresses were complete, followed by a phone call, a text message, and a smoke signal. The couple admitted to having laid low through the New Year. However, now we were in a pickle. The stationery designer was on vacation and had chosen to travel at a time when she didn't have any pending stationery commitments. And when she returned, her schedule was on task to cover stationery projects that were due in January, not ones that were contractually due in early December of the previous year. Within forty-eight hours of sending the e-mail, and after a timeline update from the stationery designer and Pamela Hewlett Events, the bride wanted to know if her invitations had gone out. Wait, what?! I was utterly confused, and I had to scour my emails to ensure that I had in fact communicated the updates to the couple as a result of the delay on their end in sending their guest addresses.

Due to the delay, the couple had to forego the option of handwritten calligraphy. Albeit a still-gorgeous script, this meant that the addresses were literally print-copied onto the envelopes from the couple's completed spreadsheet, which they had previously approved. In this situation, the bride was adamant that her current address be used as the return address for the invitations—an address that she unexpectedly chose to move from just one month after the invitations were mailed out. We sometimes receive returned invitations from the post office weeks, and sometimes months, after a wedding takes place, so, yes, I know, I know, "Run, Pam, Run!"

As a wedding planner, you can choose your battles. If you decide to offer RSVP management services, make certain that you communicate exactly how it works, as well as what your business does and does not have control over. The bride was convinced that we were at fault for invitations that didn't reach some of their guests, but we later learned that the couple had either transposed digits or recorded some of their guests' addresses incorrectly. Wedding planners are often tasked with explaining that not only do we not work for the United States Postal Service, but also that we have no control over the life of that invitation once it leaves our hands and becomes the property of the Postal Service, who is responsible for physically delivering the invitations to each guest.

The Bridal Shower

This piece is rather short, but I thought it worth sharing as it fits into other parts of this story that you'll soon read about. Sounds pretty serious, right? Whelp, it is. My goal is to help you learn from my mistakes. I want you to understand that the word "no" is a complete sentence— and that it is okay to say it with confidence. I also hope that you will discover your worth, much sooner than I did, if you haven't already.

When you quote your prices or share your package information, it is wise to include a list of additional services that you offer for an additional cost—sort of like an à la carte menu of services. This can include things like bridal showers, rehearsal dinners, and bachelor or bachelorette weekends. This list should include sourcing or planning for any additional items or activities that you may be called upon for but that are not included in your wedding planning packages or signed contract.

The bride's godmother and sister were set to plan the bridal shower. My contact information was passed along to the sister to ensure I was an invited guest. However, somehow it was communicated that I could be utilized as a resource for planning the bridal shower. I made the mistake of not putting a stop to it when it started, which resulted in demands that I should never have been made responsible for. At one point during the shower, the sister said, "Pam, I thought I was going to have to call and curse you out, if I didn't find what I was looking for and you didn't call me back." Right then, my companion who had accompanied me to the bridal shower turned to me and said, "You are going to have problems with that one, and you cannot travel to this wedding alone." Ever heard the saying, "There is power in words?"

The Wrinkled Gown

I arrived at the resort two days before the wedding. Upon arrival, the couple, the on-site planner, and I enjoyed a pleasant tour of the wedding space, followed by a peaceful beachside meal. Although we'd experienced some initial hiccups, I felt so happy and at peace that our seven-and-a-half months of work were going to materialize as they should. Unfortunately, those happy thoughts quickly diminished when the bride's family and friends started to arrive for the couple's wedding weekend.

When I took the bride and her matron of honor out for bridal salon visits, I was sure to advise them to consider the climate in which the wedding would be taking place. I was also sure to remind them that the resort the couple had chosen for their wedding did not offer any dry cleaning or laundry services. The bride chose a gown that would easily wrinkle when folded or transported—say, when packed for a plane ride. Because the couple had planned to arrive days prior, I adamantly advised that her gown should be hung in the bathroom immediately upon arrival, which would give the gown a full three days to breathe and loosen. She was proud to share that if she did anything at all, it would be to care for and protect her wedding gown.

She didn't listen. The couple stayed off-site, where the gown remained packed and suffocated until they checked into the resort where the wedding was to be held. When the bride's family arrived and saw her wrinkled wedding gown, the onslaught of calls to me started. The bride called me to inquire about laundry services and wedding-gown care because her gown was so wrinkled she didn't know if she'd be able to wear it. I was fully aware of the results, but I called my resort contact anyway, who offered the use of the hand steamer used to steam their table linens. Despite my concerns about the dress getting water spots from the steamer, I asked that it be delivered to the bride's suite anyway. Shortly after, I received a call from the bride, who was confused about why the steamer had been accidentally delivered to her room instead of mine. Say what now?! Wedding-gown care is a service that our company didn't offer then, nor will it ever offer in the future.

Relatedly, early in my wedding planning career I didn't find much value in bridal fashion stylists. I should be able to do it all, right? Well, this is when I learned how wrong I had been. A bridal fashion stylist would have provided invaluable services to this particular client. We work with some amazing bridal salons, but we can't forget that bridal salons employ salespeople. They aren't necessarily as concerned that your gown is beach or travel-ready as they are with their sales commissions. A bridal fashion stylist would assist the bride with selecting a gown that was travel, photo, and climate friendly. When faced with unique situations, I implore you to refer your client to those who specialize in the areas in which you are inept.

Welcome Bags

Considering the intimacy of the wedding, I suggested that we distribute the welcome bags during the rehearsal dinner, which was slated to take place the day before the wedding. However, on several occasions, the bride communicated that not every person attending the dinner would receive an individual bag. Therefore, the welcome bags should be distributed privately to each guest's respective room the evening before. Prior to the wedding, I was asked to assist with this task, to which I happily agreed. The bride planned to transport an entire suitcase filled with items needed for the welcome bags, and her future sister-in-law was responsible for bringing the remainder of the necessary items. The planner in me asked, "Do you think you can get the items to me a few weeks before we are scheduled to depart for the wedding? That way I can just ship all of the items directly to the resort and retrieve them upon arrival. This way, neither of you will have the hassle of trying to transport the extra baggage." (That was me making an effort to control the situation and to prevent the headache I still ended up getting.) The bride would not hear of it, fearful that the items wouldn't all arrive. She promised that she had it under control and that the welcome bags would be ready to distribute when I arrived. I know, I know, "Why'd she hire a wedding planner, right?"

Upon arrival and after our walk-through, my first question was, "Where are the welcome bags?" To which the bride responded with a slap to her head, "I haven't even started them yet. I am waiting for my sister-in-law to bring the rest of the items, but she's on her way in the next few hours. We haven't even signed the letters that need to go into the bags yet." I thought to myself, "No biggie. I'm here to help." I suggested that she bring the items from their suite to my suite, and I asked her to let me know when the rest of the items arrived. I'd organize the bags and drop the additional items in once they arrived. The bride apologized for not having gotten started, but she was relieved that now her only task would be to sign the letters. She was ecstatic to rid her space of the two suitcases that housed some of the items needed for the gift bags, and I was happy to give her some relief.

When we opened the luggage, there was a mass of items. A quick scan revealed that the number of items were disproportionate to the total number of guests listed to receive a welcome bag. I asked, "I know each guest isn't set to receive a bag, but will each bag contain the same items?" She laughed and responded, "Oh, some of these items are leftover from the engagement party"—that Pamela Hewlett Events did not plan—"and so those items should go into the bags of the guests who didn't attend." To my wedding planners, can you guess my next question? Yep. "Do you have a copy of that guest list?" Y'all know what she said, right? "No." I told her, "No worries. We'll figure it out."

At this time, I'd received a copy of the list from the front desk of all of the couple's guests who'd already checked in, those scheduled to check in, and the corresponding suite numbers. The couple departed my suite with a promise to have the signed letters and the additional items to me later in the day, at which point I could start to hand-deliver the welcome bags to guests. Later in the day never came. Even with follow-up phone calls, text messages, and a physical visit to the couple's empty suite, later in the day never came. I spent the evening preparing the bags with what we had available.

The next morning, the day of the rehearsal dinner, I set out to retrieve the signed letters and the remaining items needed to complete the welcome bags, to ensure that they were delivered to each designated guest before the rehearsal began, per the bride's request. (Please note that by day the average temperature was 102 degrees, and the welcome bags were to be hand-delivered to each guest's suite.) I was unable to reach the couple by phone or by visiting their room. With that, and the checklist up-to-date on my end, we were at somewhat of a standstill. With a forfeiture of dinner the night before—substituting with delivery of the best cold cardboard pizza I'd ever had in my life (yum)—I decided to venture out to breakfast for a real meal. Shortly after I returned to the resort, and after attempting to reach the couple once more, they finally surfaced at around noon with the remaining items and the signed letters. With the bride's request to privately distribute all of the welcome bags before the rehearsal dinner, which was scheduled to take place in less than four hours, I knew time was of the essence.

With all of the welcome bags finally completed, I set out on foot to deliver them to the wedding guests. According to the updated list from the front desk, more than half the guests still hadn't arrived. Although we were short on time, I was able to successfully deliver welcome bags to those who had arrived, with minor incident. However, imagine showing up to deliver a single welcome bag to a suite, unaware that you'd have to face a number of other suite occupants and wedding guests wanting to know "Where is mine?" I thought, "Aha! There's the trick bag!"

After several calls to the front desk for an update on guest arrivals, one of the attendants I'd become pretty familiar with, and who was now aware of the bride's special distribution request, had a suggestion. The resort was huge, all of the guests had yet to arrive, and the start time for the wedding rehearsal and dinner was rapidly approaching. She kindly asked if the bags were pre-addressed. After sharing that the bags were in fact addressed to specific guests, she asked if it would be okay for her and the rest of the ladies at the front desk to lend a hand. I happily agreed to have a houseman drive over to my suite with a cart, load the welcome bags up, and deliver them to the front office, where she would distribute them to each of the remaining designated guests upon arrival. Voilà! Problem solved, right? Think again.

After the wedding rehearsal was completed, we headed up the boardwalk for the rehearsal dinner, and it appeared that many of the wedding guests had arrived. Everyone, including the bride and groom, seemed to be having a wonderful time. It was almost as if things were too calm for the bride, because I overheard her asking some of their guests if they'd received their welcome bag. I figured my ears were obviously deceiving me. I learned I was wrong when the bride scurried over to me at the rehearsal dinner to ask where the rest of the welcome bags were because some of the guests were saying they didn't receive one yet. I shared with her the arrangement I'd made with the front desk to distribute the remaining welcome bags, including to those who had yet to arrive. She said, "Well, can you have them bring them here?"

Wait a minute! Hold up! Is this the same bride who was adamant that these bags not be distributed at the very event at which we were standing? Guess who called my wonderful new friend at the front desk to request that the welcome bags be delivered to the rehearsal dinner? She said to me, "Really? It's actually going well up here. I've already unloaded six of them. Are you sure?" With the bride directly in front of me, I replied, "Yes, please. The bride has changed her mind." The welcome bags were delivered, and I watched the bride run around the rehearsal dinner distributing welcome bags. I couldn't believe what I was seeing. My original suggestion to distribute the welcome bags at the rehearsal dinner, which the bride adamantly declined, was taking place right in front of my eyes. Can you guess who still ended up toting over a dozen of the welcome bags back to her suite for guests who still had yet to arrive?

These welcome bags were an issue all the way through the end of the wedding reception. That was the one thing the bride would speak to me about—to ask me about leftover welcome bags that some guests had yet to receive. Thankfully, I am always pretty organized, and I can access any lists connected to each wedding at any moment. I was able to inform the bride that some of the names she was asking me about were names not included on the list that she provided to receive a welcome bag. Wedding planners, I don't need to summarize the lesson here, right? You've already identified how I should have handled these welcome bags differently, right? Even as far back as the "no" that should have been issued when the original request was made, right? Awesome! Great job!

Wedding Planning: The Glam & The Glum

The following morning, the day of the wedding, I received an unannounced visit from the bride's sister, the maid of honor. She arrived with a request from the bride for me to hand-deliver special gifts to the groom, specifically after he was dressed and when the photographer was present, but without capturing the gift itself in the photos. It was my first time hearing the request, but I happily accepted and assured her that it would be taken care of. The second request was from the sister herself, who told me that the bride had been stressed the day before. I inquired about why she was stressed, to which she responded, "Well, the situation with the gift bags, her wedding gown, and stuff like that," to which I responded with what was probably considered a blank stare. She followed up with how I knew her sister liked to be in control of everything, and she requested that I hold her sister's hand throughout the day. When I saw the bride doing more than she should or getting too stressed out, her sister asked me to stop her and offer to do it for her. Yep! Imagine Pam's big ole balloon-sized eyeballs, mouth in an O, and eyes crossed at this request!

I kindly shared that I didn't believe I could control her sister being stressed or which tasks she decided to take on. I advised that I would be stopping in periodically throughout the day to check in on her sister and to make vendor introductions as they arrived to her suite, but that the special request to hold her sister's hand would not be accommodated. I politely escorted her to the door, sharing that I needed to get started on the pre-arranged timeline for this special and important day for her sister and her fiancé.

Calling All Guests

Speaking of the timeline . . . Organized wedding planners usually like to create a detailed day-of timeline for the wedding day, that includes everything from breakfast and bathroom breaks to photos and pre-wedding prayers. You name it, it's listed! It's a great resource for the wedding planner, the couple, the wedding vendors, the venue, and even the wedding party. Well, the bride decided to share her printed version of the timeline with all of her friends and family who were gathered in her suite on the day of the wedding. By now, I believe word had gotten around that I'd declined the bride's sister's early-morning request. They literally tore the timeline apart and had commentary or questions about everything listed on the timeline, including the line item titled, "Guest Seating." Any time I've shared this story with others, they ask, "Didn't all the guests receive a wedding invitation?" Most wedding guests know they should arrive several minutes prior to the listed start time to take their seats before the ceremony.

We were on schedule, and the day-of tasks were coming together perfectly, just as planned. During one of my trips over to the wedding reception area, I was stopped in transit by one of the bride's godsisters and one other young lady, whom I don't recall being familiar with. Neither were a part of the wedding party. They had a copy of the timeline I'd created in hand. ("Hey, where'd ya get that?") They wanted to know if I was planning to contact all of the guests by phone to advise them that guest seating would be available approximately fifteen minutes before the wedding started. I asked why I would do that. They shared that the timeline I had created blocked off time for guest seating before the scheduled start of the ceremony, but that none of the guests knew about it. I asked if there were guests present who had not received an invitation and who therefore wouldn't know what time to arrive. (What person would fly to a foreign island specifically to attend a wedding and not know what time it starts?) They were adamant that I contact each one, via phone, to make all guests aware of the time I had scheduled for guest seating. I responded, "No."

Shortly after the encounter and after I'd continued to my destination, I received a call from the bride asking why I was not willing to call all of her guests. I told her I'd stop by shortly to speak to her. When I arrived to the suite, the tension was so thick it could be cut with a knife. With the timeline (which she and I had reviewed a week prior) in hand and what looked like the threat of tears, the bride started ranting about how her guests were not going to know that guest seating would be taking place approximately fifteen minutes before the wedding. I explained that each of her guests had received an invitation to the wedding, which listed the start time of the wedding ceremony. I also explained that the couple's names, along with the start time of the wedding, was listed around the resort on portable monitors with a wish of congratulations. I shared that the timeline was really just a reference and a courtesy for all of us working to keep us on schedule and that her guests would understand the common knowledge that they needed to arrive a bit early.

She would not hear of it, and she explained that she had family members who were always late for things and that if I didn't call them, they wouldn't know when to arrive to the wedding. The voice inside my head thought, "So, they are going to be late with or without a call, yes?" The friend who'd made the request to me about making calls to the guests was breathing figurative fire on the side of my face, her hands on her hips. She said, "Well, you're her wedding planner, so you should be doing what she is asking you to do," to which I happily responded, "You seem to be really interested in helping your friend; perhaps you can take on this task."

My response was not a favorable one. However, not only was there no time for such a task, but it was also not something we had previously agreed to and it wasn't in our contract. If so, we would have sectioned off time in the day specifically for it. Wedding planners certainly take on many new, unexpected challenges and requests on the day of weddings, but this was such a foreign request—and one that I already knew would be a waste of time. The bride's friend took the copy of the guest list I'd retrieved from the front desk, and she called all of the guests—only to have about a third of the guests either not show up or arrive so late, that they had to watch from the boardwalk.

Hair & Makeup

There are a great number of wedding-industry professionals that serve this industry because passion led them here, while others are true salespersons. It is important that clients and wedding planners build respectable, trusting relationships with each other. When this happens, both parties start to protect one another, in a sense.

Early on in my wedding planning career, I thought it was innovative to secure a different or new set of vendors for each wedding. Over time, I learned why some wedding planners choose the same vendors for almost every event. Well, it works! Nothing runs better than a well-oiled machine.

Long before the date of our departure, we sought out and contracted one of the most highly recommended beauty salons in the area, who offered on-location wedding day bridal services. We secured services with a 50 percent deposit, with the remaining balance to be paid after the completion of services on the day of the wedding. I must give the bride credit for her willingness to always ensure that balances were paid in advance of the due date. She requested that I hold on to the remaining balance for the beauty services that were to be rendered on the day of the wedding so she wouldn't have to lift a finger. I advised her that she would just need to have a credit card handy to pay the salon's final balance for the beauty services rendered.

Oftentimes, the initially selected beauty options may change on the day of service—for instance, if the bride elects to get lash or hair extensions, which would increase the balance owed to the salon. In this instance, there wouldn't be a formal trial run of the beauty services prior to the wedding, so there was a huge possibility that services might change or increase. The bride didn't want to have to worry about anything and insisted on transferring those funds to my company. I reluctantly accepted and held on to the funds for the beauty services. At the time, I didn't offer the option to make direct vendor payments on behalf of my clients, so these funds were held in a separate debit account. We contracted beauty services for four individuals: the bride, the matron of honor, and two junior bridesmaids.

The salon providing the beauty services showed up to the resort well-prepared but, in my humble opinion, over-equipped and ready to upsell their services. When they arrived, there was already a bashing session taking place in my honor, due to my refusal to meet those earlier non-contractual demands of ironing wedding gowns, phoning all guests, or controlling the bride's human nature to take on tasks that she didn't need to take on. The lovely beauty professionals saw this as an opportunity to join in on the fun, offering comfort to the upset bride, as well as additional beauty services to individuals who were not part of the wedding party or the initial service agreement. In addition to the services provided to the four ladies who were contracted to receive beauty services, Grandma, Mom, a cousin, a best friend, an aunt, and the groom's sister all received both hair and makeup services, increasing the remaining $350 balance to over one thousand dollars. That's not really a big deal for a bridal party, right? Wrong!

Remember that debit account mentioned earlier that contained the funds to cover the remaining balance? The one that Pamela Hewlett Events did not want to retain? Yes, the card attached to that account was provided to the beauty salon to keep on file to cover the remaining balance, and yep, you guessed it—said card declined! Can you guess what happened next? Yep, the entire bridal support system went into an uproar because "You've already paid for all of this, so your wedding planner must have spent your money! Where is she?! We will handle this for you at once!"

One member of the crafty beauty team, a cousin, and a best friend came barreling across the resort grounds to the opposite side of the resort, where I was overseeing wedding day setup details, to converge on me and to inform me that the bride was upset because I'd disappointed her, yet again. At this point, I was sweating bullets from the heat and now from the trio before me (none of whom were listed on the contract between the clients and Pamela Hewlett Events). I was so completely confused about what was going on, and at that point I was nervous and starting to feel embarrassed. I assumed that my completing a transaction in a foreign location had triggered a fraud alert that must have caused the decline because surely there were enough funds to cover the remaining balance. After the hair stylist from the salon informed me of the newly acquired outstanding balance, my jaw dropped because there were decidedly not enough funds available on this particular card to cover it.

My first thought was that the bride was fully aware of how much she had in reserves for beauty services. My second thought was, "Pam, you should have stood on your no." What on earth occurred in that room, and why would she allow this attack on me to occur? I attempted to reach her on her cell phone, to no avail, and then I tried her room, only to be told that the bride was busy getting dressed. Although it rarely occurs, we are usually fully prepared to handle any financial responsibilities, within reason, that may arise on behalf of our clients on their wedding day, in which case we would just bill them later. Although we hadn't experienced any payment delays or issues with the clients, the shift in the bride's personality, the rising tensions, the sudden case of memory loss, and—last but certainly not least—the amount of the overage all gave me pause about covering this balance with my own company funds.

As always, I was wearing a crossbody bag. It housed my resort key, driver's license, personal debit card, and a little cash. If anyone is familiar with Chase Bank, they will halt you in your tracks if you swipe your personal debit card in a foreign place. That's exactly what happened when I attempted to cover the balance. However, due to the lack of Wi-Fi connectivity in the banquet area, I didn't receive the "blink once if it's you, blink twice if it isn't you" email from Chase Bank. In an attempt at keeping the peace and allowing the bride to get dressed in a timely manner, I hightailed it across the resort to my suite to retrieve my business credit card, on which I was able to cover the remaining balance for the bride and her bridal-day support team. To cover myself, I sent a brief note to the bride via text and email, describing her financial obligation for the additional beauty services rendered. Yep, you guessed it—she was pissed. However, none of this should have ever occurred. I should never have placed my company in a position to be held accountable for those services or the funds to cover such an overage.

The Rest of the Story

After the wedding reception was underway, the bride's sister, who stood up as the maid of honor, started to get very "happy." She invaded my personal space by hanging and hugging on me, and slurring her thoughts of love and thanks toward me, directly in my face. She explained that although she wanted to beat me up earlier in the day, I had done an excellent job. This took place along with two of her sidekicks, with one literally on either side of her, carrying on in a similar manner. I felt so uneasy and, honestly, unsafe.

At this point, the bride chose to ignore my attempts to interact with her in an effort to complete the remaining items listed on the wedding reception schedule—moments that couples usually like captured by the photographer. My amazing photographer, whom I'd built a wonderful relationship with, had noticed the hostility throughout the day. He had even walked in on the expletives being yelled in my honor when he first arrived to the bride's suite to capture preparation photos. He was so taken aback and uncomfortable with what he was witnessing, he immediately phoned me to see if I was okay and if it was safe for him to proceed. With a copy of the timeline previously sent to him, he was kind enough to literally follow me around with his camera to capture those remaining important moments, when he noticed that the bride was blatantly ignoring me. He explained to the groom that if these remaining items weren't completed, he didn't want them to be upset with either of us for not being able to furnish photos for moments that the bride was basically refusing to participate in.

At that point, I just wanted the fireworks show and farewells to occur so I could get the heck out of there! The on-site planner had departed for the day, but she was sure to have a houseman on duty to stay with me until the reception space was emptied of all wedding participants and to personally escort me back to my suite. Needless to say, I was out of there on the first thing smoking back toward Chicago the following morning. I was so grateful that other obligations prevented me from booking the extra day, which I normally do at the conclusion of destination weddings serviced by Pamela Hewlett Events.

While waiting at the airport, I received the most heartfelt email of gratitude from the groom's mother on a job well done. She and some of the other family members had picked up on some of the tension the evening before. Even though she played no part in it, she wanted to express her apologies for any difficulties I had encountered. While her message was thoughtful and appreciated, I still couldn't help but think to myself, "After all these years of doing what I love so much, is this what I signed up for? Are experiences like these my reward?"

Later, when the photos were available, I wrote a blog post, free of anything connected to the negative experience. This once again set the bride off into an onslaught of social media insults and bullying on all of my social media platforms. She commented on one of the posts with a snippet of my formal contract that states, "We will not share any of your information or property without permission." As always, prior to sharing them, I was sure to obtain written consent from the photographer, who legally owned the photographs. A couple has every right to request that their photographs not be shared publicly. However, that was not the case here because the photos included in our blog feature had already been publicly shared multiple times by individuals outside of the bride and groom, including some of the other wedding vendors. Needless to say, our contract now includes a clear and detailed clause regarding photograph sharing.

More than three months later, the bride was again unhappy with me for not acquiescing to yet another of her demands. When she publicly threatened to sue my company, right on social media, I publicly requested that she pass my information along to her attorney, which took her over the edge. I am not certain what she had expected me to say, but I'd had it with her and the temper tantrums. At that point, I knew not to speak another word to her, publicly or privately. I was also aware that individuals who publicly threaten, usually privately cower.

She went on to spend the entire day attempting to defame Pamela Hewlett Events. The one thing about her public outburst that made me so proud is that in every single post, she was sure to state, "And I wouldn't hire her to plan a one-year-old's birthday party. All she kept mentioning was her contract when asked to complete the simplest requests by me or my family. All she kept saying was, 'You are not on the contract' or 'That is not covered on our contract.'" Bingo! This, my friends, is why it is so important to have a written contract in place for your business. Even when you have revised it, as often as I have mine, it protects you, your business, and your brand. Even though she made public threats, I didn't expect it to go anywhere beyond social media. However, with social media as the driving force behind almost everything now, we know that this is the sort of thing that can in fact really hurt you or your business's reputation. Although she failed to mention that there were no asks or requests made by her, or on her behalf (only demands), I thought it very kind of her to publicly admit that these requests were made outside of the contract that she, the groom, and I had all signed. Her Freudian slip worked in my favor.

There were so many signs that pointed to this very result, including the admission of a detail that was shared with me during our final follow-up meeting. The bride informed me that a family member needed to be removed from the guest list as the result of a physical altercation between herself and the family member. The altercation had ensued because the bride's sister-in-law had made a comment on the upcoming travel arrangements to the wedding that the bride felt was negative or inappropriate. She admitted that she didn't know what had come over her, as it was unlike her, but that she had in fact initiated the fight. Although this series of events did take place surrounding the wedding, I was shocked to learn that she'd been in a physical altercation, and only a few weeks prior to the date of her wedding. The bride confided that she was remorseful and embarrassed afterward.

When I returned from the wedding, I sent a follow-up email to the bride and groom, detailing the events that occurred, along with a duplicate copy of the contract. I'd also sent a separate email and invoice for the outstanding balance that I'd covered for the overage in beauty services provided to the bride's family members, which was now immediately payable to Pamela Hewlett Events. Upon their return from their honeymoon, the groom immediately responded with payment and a request for a duplicate copy of the original invoice, detailing the beauty services to be provided and to whom.

I love every single one of my couples, past and present, as they have each brought meaningful relationships, experiences, and lessons to my life as a small business owner and wedding planner. With that, we are all only one person. We can only do so much. Cater to your clients, tend to them, be available to them, but ensure that you communicate both orally and in writing that you are not a personal assistant and that you cannot spend their entire wedding day both tending to their personal needs and executing a flawless wedding day for them and all of their guests. It is perfectly fine to offer personal aide services, to be provided by someone on your staff, for an additional cost. It is even better to recommend early on that the bride designate a cousin, aunt, or family friend as their personal aide or assistant for the day. You can even detail some of the things that they might need to call on the personal aide for.

Many new requests and ideas that tend to surface on the day of a wedding are outside of the list of services included in a couple's wedding package and contract. Many of these requests and ideas are not always from parties who have signed or been included in the contract. Oftentimes, we as wedding planners jump in to save the day and to place a check mark next to a task, because it's what we do. When it's all said and done, our truest desire is to do what's best for our brides and grooms. We want them to be happy and at peace on their wedding day. However, it is important to communicate that the purpose of hiring a wedding planner is to plan every detail leading up to the conclusion of the day-of wedding festivities. You are not a gofer to anyone, and especially not to individuals who have not hired you. Maintaining open communication throughout the entire wedding planning process ensures that you're not expected to leave a very important post for a safety pin. Couples sometimes request that wedding planners go and grab Aunt Ruth (whom you have never laid eyes on) for a photo op. Because we love what we do and never want to disappoint our clients, we say, "Ok, yes, will do," just as cheerfully as we say, "No, of course not," when they ask us if it's going to rain on their wedding day.

It took me the longest to write this chapter for a few reasons. Initially, it was painful to recollect these moments, but I quickly realized that it was therapeutic to write it all out. I also wanted to be sure not to cheat you of one single detail of this story, in the hopes that someone would learn from some of my mistakes, just as I have.

Chapter 3

You, Too, Can Choose

Some future brides and grooms hire wedding planners strictly based on referrals, which we love. Then there are some who hire based on countless hours of research and vetting, which they should, as they are preparing to make an investment into their future together.

We often forget—especially in the early stages of our wedding planning careers—that we, too, have the power and the right to choose our clients. Just as potential clients are interviewing you, to determine if you're a good fit for them, you should also conduct an in-depth interview of your own, to determine if they are a good fit for you and your brand.

When I first started receiving requests to plan weddings, I agreed to certain requests on a volunteer basis because I had organically developed a love for wedding planning. Then I graduated to allowing couples to give me a token of appreciation. In the past—the far, far past—I have received a hundred-dollar gift card to Olive Garden, three-hundred dollars in cash, and a special recognition in front of all the wedding guests. And I cannot forget my all-time favorite: I was once allowed to take not one but two of the leftover wedding favors (glass coasters engraved with the couple's names and wedding date) for my own personal use. I am eternally grateful for each of my starter clients. Not only did they take a chance on me, but I was afforded the opportunity to see what it really takes to plan an elaborate wedding or celebration for my own personal satisfaction and fulfillment, versus the hope of recognition by wedding bloggers and social media.

I learned so much on my own through trial, error, tears, and triumphs. Those early experiences built the confidence that I now proudly carry. They taught me my worth as a wedding planner and led me to share my past struggles with wedding planners who come along after me. I also learned that I can help and share, but that I don't have to feel bad for not passing on any proprietary information connected directly to my business.

I also learned to discern potential clients who approach me but don't have any intentions on becoming my client—or that of any other wedding planner. The most important lesson those early experiences taught me is that I reserve the right to choose who I work for and with. As I have continued to grow as a wedding planner, I have learned (sometimes the hard way) that not every signed agreement was for Pamela Hewlett Events. It is important to identify your ideal client. Although I took a break from wedding planning, I knew that my experiences and tests in this business would only make me stronger. When I determined my worth and who I wanted to work with, I earnestly prayed that God would lead me to my ideal clients. Wedding planners and business owners in any other field, I implore you to identify every detail of your ideal client. This will improve your ability to identify key details that will increase your level of comfort when communicating during initial conversations or consultations. Determine your worth and where you want your business to go. This will save you a lot of heartaches and headaches.

Because I started Pamela Hewlett Events after a rash of volunteer efforts for both social and nonprofit clients and events, I struggled with asking some of the most important questions that could have potentially saved me a lot of time and money. I was, for example, afraid to talk about money. I didn't ask about clients' budgets. I underquoted the prices of my services and the services of other vendors. I once even allowed a client to book a venue where the walls were so unattractive that I ended up investing my own funds to add class and elegance to the space. But I loved what I was doing, right? I was trying to build my portfolio, right? So I accepted the experience and the losses with an *S* on my chest.

Then one day a light bulb went off, almost immediately after encountering a set of clients who, without pause, demanded that I perform a six-figure budget wedding on a very low five-figure budget. The light bulbs did not stop there. Long after I established Pamela Hewlett Events, I had a pair of clients (or two, or three) who lowballed their true budget by over 50 percent. Guess who had discounted their service rate to sign the client and also did not have a clause in her contract regarding budget minimums and maximums? Yep, you guessed it! The very person whose words you're reading.

Once you spend over two hundred and fifty underappreciated and underpaid hours planning an elaborate wedding celebration, it becomes easier to identify the ideal client for your business. It becomes easier to determine during initial phone consultations—and prior to spending hundreds of dollars on fancy beverages, scones, lunches, and dinners—if you are speaking to your ideal client. I am a fan of meeting face-to-face, and I believe each business owner should budget for the occasional coffee, lunch, or dinner meeting, but I am also a fan of saving time, for both potential clients and for myself.

We all hit bumps on our journey in business, especially as small business owners. During those moments when the phone is not ringing and the inquiries are not coming in via email, desperation can often surface. During these times, we might find ourselves taking on a client that ends up being an expense to us, in more ways than one. This can happen when we underquote to win business, or because we accepted a client whose budget was not in line with our ideal client. You can almost always assume the wedding planner will invest more resources than those listed within the signed agreement. However, it should never hurt you or your bank account.

Always remember that as you are being chosen, you should also be choosing. Taking on a client who admires your work but can't truly afford your services might not be the best idea for your business. This is not being mean. It's protecting your brand and peace of mind.

It is important to build relationships with other wedding planners. The role of a wedding planner has so much variety to it, that ten wedding planners in the same city might all provide completely different services. Networking and building these relationships has given me the chance to share opportunities with other wedding planners. Even though a client may not be your ideal client, you can still refer them to another wedding planner in your network. I am often approached by aspiring wedding planners or those with newly established businesses. I have referred clients to many of them. They have all been extremely grateful, as the referral turned out to be the perfect marriage. (Get it? Marriage? Okay, never mind, but I'm sure you have absorbed my message.)

I just recently stopped editing my contract as often as I used to. Before determining my ideal client and becoming confident enough to say, "Based on all of the information you've provided, I may not be a good fit for you," I found myself constantly editing my contract at the conclusion of each wedding. I always learned new information about what I did not offer, what I should offer, what I did not want to offer, and what I was offering at my own expense but what should have been paid for by the client. Record your experiences, determine your ideal client, and never discount your worth.

I love my clients. I repeat, I absolutely love my clients. I am attached to them, and many are attached to me long after their wedding is over. On average, we work with couples anywhere between twelve and eighteen months. When you work with a couple for this amount of time, you develop a unique relationship with them. A wedding is usually the largest investment a couple will make for their future together. The wedding planning process for a luxury, upscale wedding—or any wedding—can include upwards of twenty wedding vendors. The wedding planning process entails hundreds of details and decisions, from stationery verbiage and patterns and inserts for wedding invitations to DJs and band playlists, all of which fall as the wedding planner's responsibility. Initial conversations and vigorous note-taking between you and your client are key elements to the wedding planning process. Gleaning these details will help answer any questions your clients' prospective wedding vendors may have before signing a contract. Working with so many wedding vendors entails an immense amount of communication between you, your clients, and each wedding vendor.

You should incorporate the tools and knowledge acquired in corporate America into your businesses. Many of us who have the desire to leave corporate America want more freedom, flexibility, and the option to pursue our dreams. However, I do not believe you should leave corporate America to start your business, only to be forced into facing the same challenges that caused you to leave in the first place. So many wedding planning publications, blogs, and conferences teach that we should empty our tanks to obtain and to please clients, and that we should do everything they ask of us. What we are not taught is the worth and price point of such services, or that we are in control as the bosses of our businesses. Or that if it is not in our contract, we are not obligated to fulfill the request. And lastly, I have never read in our industry that it is okay to say no when, sometimes, that is the only possible answer.

Chapter 4

The Best Ideas Are Your Own Ideas, Right?

When you truly learn and grow from your experiences as a small business owner, it becomes easier to expound and to be transparent in sharing those experiences. I am guilty of having thought, at one point, that sharing tips and advice meant giving away all of my hard work. As I continued to grow spiritually, and as I brought God into my business as I had with every other component of my life, I quickly realized that *that* couldn't be further from the truth. In reality, one of the greatest accomplishments that a person or small business owner can achieve in their own business is for an aspiring, or even current business owner in your industry to approach you and ask, "How?"

Granted, I've worked extremely hard to grow my business, and I would be a fool to give away the whole cow for free. However, over time, as I've continued to connect with other successful female entrepreneurs, either through networking events, developing business-BFF relationships, or by simply subscribing to their podcasts, I've observed that they all had two major character components in common: (1) They are believers and women of faith, and (2)

They each had a willingness to be transparent in sharing the successes, pitfalls, setbacks, and mistakes they've experienced in their individual journeys as entrepreneurs and small business owners. They've also shared the effects that running their businesses have had on their personal lives.

Monique Rodriguez, Founder and CEO of Mielle Organics, hosts a podcast titled *The Secret Sauce to Success*. In several of the episodes, she talks about not going at it alone, even when we believe we can. We should all be inspired by someone who has surpassed the place or point we're trying to get to. We don't have to model ourselves after anyone, and we don't need to try to copy anyone else's originality, because it's just that—*their* originality, which means it's already taken. However, what we can do is use the gems we receive from others as inspiration and encouragement.

As wedding planners, we are always approached and sought out by clients who aren't the ideal client for our businesses. At some point in your career, you may notice posts on social media that appear to mirror your styles and ideas. Yep, you know exactly who's posting . . . the very individuals who made inquiries of you, but didn't want to pay for the cost of your services. Sometimes you'll find that the familiar imagery is the work of one of your friendly wedding industry peers. Not that long ago, when photos of weddings and events that appeared to mimic my work would surface from individuals who had previously inquired about my services or admired my work, I would be cayenne-pepper hot! I would repost the photos that'd I'd posted months prior, with snazzy captions like, "So glad y'all liked it, even though you didn't 'like' it." I know what you're thinking: How petty and exhausting was that?!

One day, another light bulb went off in my head. First, if they do it after me, that means I've already done it. Second, someone loved it enough to use it as inspiration, even though they weren't in a position to pay for the services offered by my company. It doesn't change or negate the fact that they did want to work with my company because they admired my work. Third, I thought to myself, "Pamela, girl, you do not own the colors pink, white, gold, purple, red, or black," which are some of the colors most commonly used in the wedding industry. When I close up shop, brides will still be selecting those colors. Lastly, who's to say that a similar vision didn't come to someone else and I just happened to execute it first? Wedding planners—both new and seasoned—will always be secretly surfing Pinterest and social media, and one day your work might be the search result.

Of course, we all more than deserve proper credit for our hard work. Of course, it is in the poorest taste for wedding-industry peers to duplicate work that is not their own for a lesser cost. Of course, a simple ask from someone offering the same service might smooth things over. The questions to ask ourselves are, What am I going to do about it? And Did I protect my product or service? Whelp, if you know you're not going to invest the funds to prove someone might be guilty of stealing from you, or if you didn't protect yourself, consider doing something to release the negative energy you feel. Create the ole shady post in the notes section of your phone to get it out of your system. Get creative and e-mail the note to yourself along with a photo of your work. Do whatever you need to do to privately release the frustration. Do your best to quickly move past your frustrations because, as entrepreneurs, we should all have learned by now that we can't afford to exhaust too much time and energy on being frustrated, especially not on those things that are completely outside of our control.

I have learned that focusing on creating more of what one might call *inspiration* soothes me. Truthfully, isn't that really how we creative entrepreneurs want to spend our time and energy—creating and perfecting the ideas we have for our businesses? There are some successful wedding planning business owners who've presented at conferences around the world and provided their services five countries over. Then they find cause to go on public social media rants because someone copied them. Protect your product and your service. Then, if you feel or can determine that someone has truly stolen from you, you can dial up your attorney and have them counsel you accordingly. If you cannot provide proof that you've been stolen from, the public rants do nothing except tarnish your brand and make it harder for the reader to determine who the fool is—you or the person you're ranting about.

Think of it this way: You didn't see Kentucky Fried Chicken getting in the middle of that fried-chicken sandwich craze between Popeyes and Chick-fil-A, did you? They quietly offered a two-for-one special on their own fried-chicken sandwich. Genius, right? Have you ever seen or heard of Beyoncé expressing her dislike for what others are doing? Or getting involved in social media beefs—or conflicts of any sort, for that matter—because a new or seasoned female entertainer or artist used her accomplishments as inspiration? Nope. And you probably never will. Beyoncé is aware that there's not another individual on the planet, nor will there ever be another individual on the planet, that could be Beyoncé. Don't think for one second that she doesn't experience mimicry. I just believe she uses it to fuel her artistry and to add more dollar signs to her empire. Remember "Lemonade"? Don't allow social media bullies or snazzy posts to scare you away from doing what you love or sharing your creativity with the world. Someone needs exactly what you have to offer.

As Melissa Butler, Founder and CEO of The Lip Bar, stated on *The Secret Sauce to Success* podcast with Monique Rodriguez, "Don't allow anyone to make you feel like you can't do something, just because someone else already does it." It is absolutely possible to put your own unique spin on a product or service that you've created. It is also possible to successfully sell and market your idea or product, even though others may try to convince you that the market is already saturated with what you have to offer.

It is also ok to work together or to offer guidance and support to someone who is starting out or trying to grow past the place, you once were. During another episode of *The Secret Sauce to Success* podcast, Monique Rodriguez touches on helping others and how if helping another business owner makes you feel as though you are taking something away from yourself or your own business, then that is operating in lack, when we should all be operating in abundance. This kind of attitude does nothing at all, except block our own Blessings. There is great fulfillment in knowing that you've helped someone else achieve a goal or to reach a certain level of success.

I am a black, female entrepreneur, which qualifies me as a double minority, which means that when I walk in the front door, I already have to work three times as hard to build and protect my business and brand. I cannot afford to waste time on being upset, frustrated, or offended by the actions of others. Every single business owner obviously has to spend time working out the kinks and getting past the entrepreneurial growing pains that come with owning a business. However, please keep at the forefront of your mind how these aspects contribute to our personal growth and to the organic growth of our businesses. These are what make entrepreneurs some of the most special and unique human beings on the planet.

Chapter 5
The Secret Societies

Hold on to your wedding bouquets! This may or may not blow you away, but guess what? Yep, there's an entire secret society of wedding-industry professionals who have already decided that they ain't letting yo new a** in! I'm sorry to be the bearer of this news. I am only the messenger, but it's true. I know this to be true because I unfortunately have had many personal encounters with these secret societies. Ohhh, but wait . . . I'm not finished. Grab your toasting flute and take a sip, because there isn't just one secret society in the wedding industry! You've got The Beginners Secret Society, The Wannabe Secret Society, and, last but certainly the most frightening, the coup de grâce, The Elite Secret Society. The Elite Secret Society is made up of experienced wedding-industry professionals, and you will find that they have a collective social media following of well over ten thousand. If you've ever seen the movie *Jawbreaker*, or the television series *Gossip Girl*, you are familiar with the exact cliques to which I am referring.

The Elite Secret Society of wedding-industry professionals will shun another wedding-industry professional at an event, then later in a passive-aggressive social media post express their lack of understanding or their offense over the idea of that same wedding-industry professional hiring someone outside of the ethnic group they both share. Some members of The Elite Secret Society expect you to bow at their feet. They expect other wedding professionals to seek them out, to extend work opportunities to them on behalf of their clients, knowing they will never return the favor or even express any gratitude for the opportunity.

The Chicago wedding market does a great job hosting networking events for wedding-industry professionals. It's a perfect opportunity to build new relationships, and I have met a number of my vendors by attending these events. The events are always so well organized, they are usually free to attend, and I always have a really fun time. However, there have been times when I admired someone or their work via social media, only to have them look down their noses at me when I attempted to introduce myself at an event. I'd heard of one such wedding planner through a mutual wedding vendor. The vendor knew I wanted to build relationships with other wedding planners, and she raved about how this particular wedding planner was great at what she does. She suggested that I attempt to connect with her. I ventured to the wedding planner's social media pages, where I learned that she was an investment banker by day and ran a full-service wedding planning business by night. I happily followed her on social media and found that I was always impressed with the work she was doing.

On one occasion, I attended the spring launch for a well-established wedding publication. Imagine my excitement when I checked in at the registration table and saw a name tag with the company name of the person I had been following and admiring for months. (Hey, that's what you do when you arrive at a networking event—or at least that's what you should consider doing. Scan the names you see. There may be someone attending that you've always wanted to meet or connect with.)

After speaking to a few people and grabbing some snacks, I asked a seated group of two if they would mind if I sat with them, as there was a total of two empty seats remaining. The first lady said that one seat was for her boss, and the other just shrugged her shoulders. I smiled and said, "Ok, I'll take just one." I went on to introduce myself as the owner of Pamela Hewlett Events. Neither seemed impressed, but I wasn't bothered, because I knew I'd only sit for a moment. Another lady approached and said, "Oh, I think I'll take that seat so I can have a better view." One of the ladies stood and offered up the seat. I assumed that this must be her boss. The lady took the seat and went on to say, "Don't forget, we have one more person we're waiting for." It took me a second to realize that I was keeping a seat warm for someone else. It was as if everything clicked at once. I noticed that there was a tent card in the center of the table, which listed the name of a company. Thinking back, the table may have been reserved and I just didn't realize it when I approached, and those seated never said a word.

The company name was of the wedding planner I had been following on social media. She, like me, uses her given name in her company name. I immediately got excited and asked those seated at the table if she was there. The new, rude lady who had taken the other woman's seat was the woman I had been admiring for months. She responded with, "That would be me," and turned her attention toward the growing crowd. I attempted to introduce myself and share that I was a fan of her work, but I was interrupted when she asked her assistant a question. I'd like to assume that she didn't hear me, but I was sitting right next to her and the noise level was still minimal at that point. I was disappointed to learn that someone I'd been following and admiring, who I thought of as a very talented wedding planner, would be so cold and unapproachable. Then I realized that this was her team and that I'd face more mean-girl tendencies by them, if I stayed any longer.

Unfortunately, I have experienced this on more than one occasion. If you are a new wedding planner, or just new to building relationships, please don't come into this industry and assume those who look like you or share the same occupation will automatically embrace you. In fact, sometimes they'll be the very ones who will purposely make you feel left out and unwelcome in what may already be a new or unfamiliar atmosphere. It is natural to gravitate toward those we believe to be similar to ourselves. However, introducing yourself to someone you might have assumed you have nothing in common with can also lead to some of the most beautiful peer relationships.

I am based in the Chicagoland area, but I have built positive relationships with some of the best wedding planners and wedding professionals in the business from all around the world. They never look down on others and, in fact, they are always willing to help others in areas that they may be struggling. These individuals are always willing to answer questions or lend a listening ear. You can find me among these individuals. We may find comfort in those we are most familiar with, but you will find that you also identify with those who you aren't necessarily familiar with. Look everywhere for your tribe, and make sure that it is made up of a variety of people from a variety of places. You may meet someone with a new wedding planning business who only has one hundred followers but, like me, holds a BA in marketing communications and an MS in hospitality management, who would serve as a great resource to you. Be open-minded, be kind, and you will build relationships in this business that will last you a lifetime.

The truth is, we will all be denied access to something at some point as an entrepreneur or wedding-business owner. The only downfall to denial would be allowing it to be a distraction, a determent, or a discouragement to your success and growth as an individual and as a wedding planner. Ask yourself what you are going to do with the rejections you receive. They are coming. Even when you are a ten- or twenty-year wedding planning veteran, the glum is coming and there's no way around it. In the story I shared above, they literally didn't want to give me a seat at the table, but there were a dozen other tables for me to choose from. I departed their table knowing that I would build my own table and that I would be much more gracious with mine. When establishing yourself as a wedding planner, I recommend following the advice of business coach Marshawn Evans Daniels: "Don't blend in...burst out."

Chapter 6
Hashtag Heaven or Hashtag Hell?

In recent years, the wedding industry has been filled with new trends, followers, likes, social media apps, blogs, publications, styled shoots, and features. All of it creates excitement and makes both the seasoned and new wedding planner more enthused about being a part of this blooming industry. While all of these components are amazing and have made this industry so much more exciting and intriguing, it has also caused discouragement. The influx of information on the wedding industry has created excitement and sometimes unnecessary competition. Many experienced wedding planners study and observe to stay abreast, while many aspiring wedding planners wonder where on earth to begin. And truthfully, I am simply over some wedding-industry professionals glamorizing the glum components of this industry in an effort to obtain followers, likes, and sometimes the obviously unideal client for their businesses.

I am extremely proud of my website and social media pages, especially since it took some trial and error before I landed in the creative hands of a talented website designer who caters to creative entrepreneurs. Numbers can either distract or encourage us when starting or maintaining a business or birthing an idea. I have had the pleasure of personally experiencing both in my business. We are living in an age when the life of some businesses are predicted solely on the existence of social media and its tricky algorithms.

When I decided to start this book, I asked myself question after question, almost to the point of completely discouraging myself from even getting started. Then I remembered that I believe in a much higher power that did not create in me a fearful spirit. My social media pages may not be filled with tens of thousands of followers or even the most glamorous of weddings the eye has ever seen. However, I have chosen to be honest with myself, so I acknowledge that someone will always be better or further along, and that's okay. What others are doing is not my focus, and it shouldn't be yours either. We will always have an opportunity to learn and grow. In fact, I will forever acknowledge those whose wedding planning businesses have exceeded where I am in my business—those who are where I'd like to be. If I don't, what exactly am I aspiring to? Either way, I knew I couldn't continue not starting to write.

Social media can determine the success or failure of a business today. It is where everyone is spending their time—even my parents! The parental unit is on social media, and I never thought I'd see the day. Sometimes I don't know how to handle my mom being more up on things than I am. Seriously, it's the cutest, funniest thing! Social media is one of the number-one resources to obtain information for both small business owners and consumers alike. We live in a world where you may sometimes feel as though you need to attend Hashtag University in order to craft the perfect post and gain some likes, or maybe even a few new followers. For years, I had no idea why so many people were using the little pound sign on the keypad after social media posts. I learned that this was called a hashtag, and I noticed these little pound signs appearing in all sorts of posts, including rants, new profile photos, new purses, shoes, cars, church sermon topics . . . everything! Then I learned that if I just clicked on one of the hashtags, a million others just like it would appear!

People with a larger following will follow you to get you to follow them, only for them to unfollow you a few days later. Sounds like a lot to have to monitor, right? It is, but it is also worth paying attention to when you have a few extra minutes in your day. Consider posting consistently, or simply following a page because it is of interest to you. This is especially important for social media business pages, where referrals, partnerships, and notoriety are often heavily based on numbers, versus quality. Please remember that while having a large number of social media followers definitely has its perks, it does not always equal a paycheck or consistent income. Honesty and authenticity will take you far in the wedding industry.

Chapter 7

Fulfilling Fairy Tales

Little girls and big little girls dream of the day that they will dress up like a princess and marry their prince. If you are one who truly enjoys making dreams come true, wedding planning might be the career for you. It is a blessing, and so fulfilling, for someone to want to hire Pamela Hewlett Events to plan their wedding. It is the most important day that two people who have found love in one another will ever share. A couple's wedding day marks the day that they will pledge their love to one another before God and in the presence of all of their loved ones. To be entrusted with every detail of such an important day, that investment into a couple's future, is not a task to be taken lightly.

Sometimes we do something so consistently that the beauty of it can be easily missed. Clients say thank you all the time, and we are always grateful for their kind words. However, when someone calls you up at the crack of dawn, just a few hours before they are scheduled to depart for their honeymoon, and says to you, "I want to go back to yesterday because I feel like I was a part of the most magical fairy tale ever" or "We were always confident that you would do a great job, pulling all of the details together; but what you actually pulled off was beyond anything we could have ever imagined," a different emotion is evoked. Although you are paid for wedding planning services, you feel something that far exceeds your title as a wedding planner. You experience what it means to be selfless, what it feels like to care about making someone else happy. You are rewarded with helping to create memories that will last for more than just one lifetime. This is my "why" and the thing that keeps me going when those glum days and experiences come.

With a passion for wedding planning, you will be able to fulfill your clients' wedding fairy tales with your eyes closed, but it takes time, confidence, patience, consistency, and lots of organization. There were times when I was recording my thoughts for this book that I considered stopping altogether. I would see a post or blog piece from another wedding planner, speaking about how amazing it is to be a wedding planner or about come what may, wedding planners are just to accept and deal with it all. I am human, so during those times, my thoughts would try to creep in, predicting how other wedding planners and wedding professionals would receive this book and if they would rake me over the coals, for sharing this short collection of my thoughts and experiences. Then I'd remembered my "why."

While I am a die-heart wedding-planning and wedding-industry fan, I wanted to share both the glam and the glum that will in fact be a part of your wedding planning career. Parts that many won't ever share. Most of what I have learned and experienced over the years, I'd never heard of until I experienced it firsthand in my own business. No one shared with me that there are just as many mean-spirited people serving in this industry as there are those with kind spirits. No one shared with me that I'm only supposed to speak highly of my job as a wedding planner. No one shared with me that in spite of having a signed contract in place, you might still be forced to deal with demands from others who are not a party to that contract. One of the most disappointing things that no one shared with me is that even though you might share your clients with other wedding vendors, some will still feel the need to treat you as if you are beneath them. This was all a part of my "why," which helped me to stay encouraged and to see volume one of *Wedding Planning: The Glam & The Glum* through to the end.

As a reminder, please don't ever become discouraged by a lack of likes or comments, assuming that they're not watching . . . They are! Someone is always watching. An aspiring wedding planner, new business owner or potential clients who can't wait for an opportunity to work with you, are all watching. Trust me, they see you and they know your every move. Stay connected to your supporters and followers so that they will know that you always have them in mind and haven't forgotten about them. Post and engage by sharing parts of your life and your business. I still have to remind myself to do this, but I am here to tell you that when you do so consistently, it works in your favor and helps your business.

If you have a business you'd like to birth, or perhaps a new product or service as an extension of your business, execute it now. There are many entrepreneurs in this wedding industry who have thousands of followers and empty bank accounts to match. Don't allow the growing number of new trends in the wedding industry or the growing number of followers attached to someone else's business scare you into not getting started. The world needs what you have to offer. I refuse to be made to feel like my transparency is a negative thing. Transparency helps you and it helps others, which is what we are all here to do. Being true contributes significantly to our growth and our businesses.

Collages are a collection of visuals, usually derived from one's own thoughts. Collages are usually imperfect and they have no special order. However, the message within a collage is usually clearly communicated. This is not a how-to book, and it bears no legal or official training on running a wedding planning business or any business. This is a collage of some of my thoughts and experiences as a wedding planner and entrepreneur. I started with almost twenty chapters, but I decided to table some of them for volume two of *Wedding Planning: The Glam & The Glum*. I wanted this book to be easy to read and somewhat entertaining. I wanted to be able to help my readers in a way that would not overwhelm you with information, but that would simply share a glimpse into both the glam and glum sides of wedding planning.

Thank you for reading my first book and for allowing me to share some of my thoughts and experiences. I still have so much more to learn, and my business, Pamela Hewlett Events, is still growing. As I continue on my journey, I am committed to continuing to share. This is only the beginning, so until next time . . .

Love & Blessings,

Pamela

Connect with Pamela:

Instagram: instagram.com/pamelahewlettevents

Facebook: https://facebook.com/pamelahewlettevents

Twitter: @phewlettevents

Website: pamelahewlettevents.com

E-mail: info@pamelahewlettevents.com

www.ingramcontent.com/pod-product-compliance
Lightning Source LLC
Chambersburg PA
CBHW070503220526
45467CB00002B/548